IMAGES OF ENGLAND

HADFIELD
AND PADFIELD

IMAGES OF ENGLAND

HADFIELD
AND PADFIELD

MARGARET BUXTON

TEMPUS

Frontispiece: Harry Buxton, *c.* 1958.

First published 2005

Tempus Publishing Limited
The Mill, Brimscombe Port,
Stroud, Gloucestershire, GL5 2QG
www.tempus-publishing.com

British Library Cataloguing in Publication Data.
A catalogue record for this book is available from the British Library.

ISBN 0 7524 3563 9

Typesetting and origination by Tempus Publishing Limited.
Printed in Great Britain.

Contents

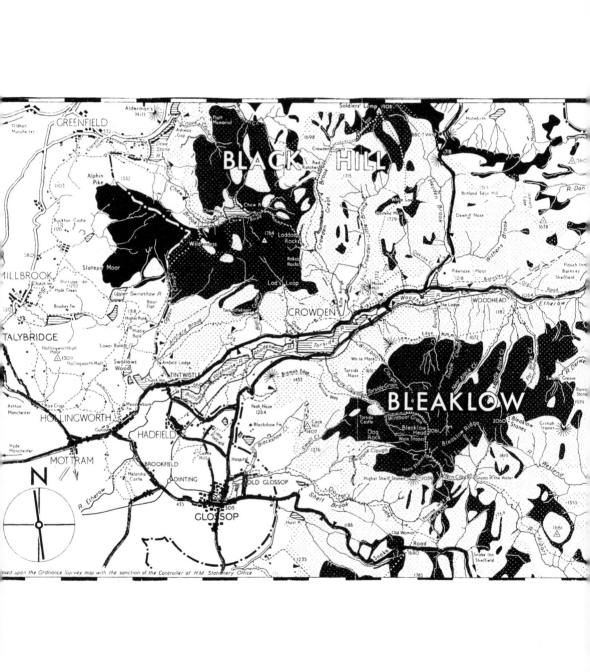

Acknowledgements

Once more it is my late father's collection of photographs that has been the inspiration for this book. He was born in Glossopdale and lived for most of his life in Hadfield, where I was born and lived for twenty-three years. My early recollections of the area are of village life. There were corner shops, few buses and our happy lives revolved around school and church, with a weekly outing to Hyde, Stockport or Manchester. As hills and green fields surrounded the area, we often walked through meadows just yards from our street - it was even possible to get to Mottram without much pavement walking. My father, Harry Buxton (1908-1983), travelled extensively into the High Peak of Derbyshire in his work as a press photographer, but he also managed to capture ordinary daily happenings locally, which have now become insights into how life used to be. After retirement he served as a councillor for Glossop Borough Council and later went to live in Whaley Bridge. I am grateful that his photographs stir up memories of how the Hadfield area used to be.

I would also like to thank Peggy Davies, Derek Bailey, Garrie Griffiths, Christine Ford and Sue Hickinson for loaning photographs for inclusion in this book.

Introduction

Hadfield and Padfield are both mentioned in the Domesday survey of England in 1086. At the time Hadfield was known as Hetfelt, an agricultural hamlet or open land where heather grew stretching across 425 acres. In the 1835 *Pigot's Commercial Directory for Derbyshire*, Hadfield was described as 'a village in the township of Hadfield and Dinting, in the parish of Glossop, about two miles away'. In the early 1400s the population was around 500; today it has risen to around 10,000 due to much redevelopment. A Manchester overspill estate was built in the sixties, older houses have been renovated and extended and many new private housing estates have been built. Also in Padfield and Woolley Bridge the population has greatly increased with the building of new houses.

In the *National Gazetteer* of 1868 it said that Hadfield was a market town in the parish of Glossop with a station on the Manchester to Sheffield railway. It also said that the River Mersey bounded the township, there were several cotton mills, quarries with good building stone and a Wesleyan chapel; market day was Thursday and fairs were held on 9 May and 15 October, chiefly for the sale of cattle.

Mouselow (or Castle Hill) was the site of a Norman castle at Hadfield and it is across the valley from the remains of the Roman fort at Melandra, near Glossop. The valley was a dense forest with roaming wild animals and became known as the 'Royal Forest of the Peak'. One of the oldest houses still standing in Hadfield dates back to 1646. Several wool and cotton mills were built on the River Etherow using the water to power machinery. A steep incline from Padfield to Castle Hill was named Redgate, after blood spilt at a battle. The Longdendale Trail, which is part of the Trans-Pennine Trail, starts near Hadfield station and was created on an old railway route to Woodhead.

Padfield used to include an area of 6,464 acres, which stretched across moorland from Padfield Brook to the Yorkshire border, and from the River Etherow to Bleaklow. Padfield Brook marked the boundary from Hadfield. It was described in a Glossop visitors guide as 'a village situated at the beginning of the Longdendale Valley in the Peak District of Derbyshire. The valley grasslands and bilberry-covered summits are densely populated by a variety of wildlife from mountain hare to grouse'. By 1811 there were seventy-eight houses and 450 people living in Padfield, and eighty-eight houses and 479 people in Hadfield.

Hadfield and Padfield were chosen as the locations for the television series 'The League of Gentlemen', which renamed the area Royston Vasey, but apart from the scenery the series bears little resemblance to the way of life in these villages. Life is now very different from many of the photographs contained in this book, but I hope it will bring back memories for those who were born and raised in the area and perhaps it will become a source of history for those who have recently come to live here.

M.M. Buxton (2005)

one

Before 1939

A gentlemen's trip in an open-topped coach from the Spread Eagle public house at Woolley Bridge, *c.* 1920. The pub had a long tradition for music, and in the late 1960s those waiting for the Hadfield bus on a Sunday night could often hear the strains of 'Danny Boy'. After a competition the pub was renamed The Riverside.

Members of Hadfield Conservative Club, standing outside their headquarters on Woolley Bridge Road, are resplendent in starched collars and watch chains, with one gentleman on the right wearing knee breeches. Notice the tramlines in the road; the tram ran from Glossop to Station Road in Hadfield via Woolley Bridge Road from 1903.

The area beyond Lambgates and between Hadfield and Padfield was known as Roughfields and was used for agriculture, keeping hens and pigeons and grazing animals. Mr Joe Swift is displaying crops that he harvested in 1925. Is it a coincidence that a leading television gardener today has the same name?

Jimmy Bennett (as Dordles the Clown) driving the horse and Joe Lomas (as Charlie Chaplain) playing a squeezebox on top of the coach. The event was a carnival in around 1927 at the top of Bank Street, on the area called the Paradise. In the background is the Old Liberal Club, where the new housing development Ewart Court has now been built.

Above: Judging by the bunting on the left in the background and the floral cross decorating the front of this fire engine, it seems likely that it too was an exhibit in the carnival procession at Bank Street. Bank Street was once known as the Strictus. The houses behind were typical early stone terraces, which were common in the village.

Left: Another entry in the carnival was this goat pulling a miniature cart bearing the inscription 'Schools & parties suppliers, Warburton, Stalybridge.' The man by the gas lamp glances at the schoolboys wearing their clogs on the cobbles of Station Road.

Opposite below: Crowds always gathered on Old Hall Square near Hadfield Cross when important news was proclaimed. Here on a cold January day in 1936 hats were doffed as the news broke of the death of George V. The clergyman, fifth from the right, is the Revd A.C.M. White, from St Andrew's church.

A Douglas 348cc twin cylinder 1921 motorcycle that used a chain and belt drive and had a top speed of 45 mph. Seated is Harry Buxton (aged nineteen), who lived at 34 Bank Street in 1927. He kept the handbrake as a memento until his old age!

St Andrew's church on a snowy day in 1936. The flag was flown at half-mast as a mark of respect for King George V. In the late 1950s a clock was erected on this side of the church grounds in memory of the Revd A.C.M. White, who had been curate, vicar and rural dean at the church for forty-six years.

The Revd Archibald Campbell MacAlastair White outside the old vicarage on Hadfield Cross, which was decorated for the Coronation of King George VI and Queen Elizabeth in 1937. Two years later the Revd White travelled on the maiden voyage of the *Mauritania* to America and Canada with Mr Wilman from Mersey Bank House.

Inside St Andrew's church, decorated to celebrate Easter in the 1930s. The church's foundation stone was laid on 30 November (St Andrew's Day) in 1872, the same year as a Church of England school opened at Waterside in Hadfield.

Opposite below: Here a proclamation is being read by Glossop's mayor John Hague in December 1936 to inform the waiting crowds of the abdication of Edward VIII. He acceded to the throne in January but could not be crowned King as he chose to marry a divorcee, Mrs Simpson.

Unlike churches over the border, Hadfield (in the Diocese of Derby) did not have Whitsuntide walks, but each May the church walked around the village on the anniversary of the Sunday school on what was known as Sermons Sunday. In Lambgates the procession usually stopped to sing the hymn 'Onward Christian Soldiers'.

The Lee memorial children's corner at St Andrew's was dedicated in September 1938. It was a gift from teachers, scholars and friends to commemorate the service of Alderman Levi Lee, who served as superintendent of the Sunday school. Local children are seen getting to grips with the language of the 1662 prayer book and the authorised version of the Bible.

Members of three Lads Brigades who competed in a band contest at Hadfield in 1939, when Flowery Field (Hyde) won the cup. The first companies were founded in 1891 in Manchester. They were an Anglican uniformed organisation that aimed to equip young people with life skills and challenges within a Christian setting. The Girls Brigade merged with the boys in 1978.

This procession of schoolchildren, on Station Road, carrying several different flags in the early 1900s is probably an Empire Day celebration. The day was known as Commonwealth Day after 1958 and was usually celebrated on Queen Victoria's birthday, 24 May. The main street was thriving at this time; both Fiddlers and Dunne's were outfitters and Pownall's and Squires sold shoes.

A dispute between the Milk Marketing Board and local farmer Mr George Brierley of Hadfield Cross led to unemployed farm workers, butchers, shopkeepers and some housewives showing their support in the 1930s. They carried a drum with the words 'In sympathy with a good farmer'.

Hadfield Library, located behind the Cenotaph, was decorated for Coronation celebrations in 1937 with a banner bearing the words 'Long live our King and Queen'. Mill owner Edward Platt funded the building. Turning the corner at the bottom of Railway Street is a horse and cart, from which milk was delivered straight from churn to jug at the customer's doors.

The library was first opened as a reading room on the lower floor in 1906. Council rents were later collected there and books could be borrowed from the middle level. As a librarian I remember only too well having to put up heavy shutters to close off the books at the end of each day! The hall above was hired out for functions.

Bankswood Park was purchased by the Corporation in 1926 and officially opened in 1931 by the mayor Herbert Lee Roebuck (seen here with town clerk Roger Rose to the right of centre). Alderman Richard (Dick) Sellers delighted the crowds by gliding down the children's banana slide at the age of fifty-eight complete with bowler hat.

Local schoolgirls wearing gymslips lined up in Bankswood Park for the choosing of a carnival queen in the 1930s. I wonder if child number six was noticed more than the others, as her number was spelt out? In the background are the railway line and the houses on South Marlow Street.

The park entrance on Park Road, also known as Marlow Brow, is situated over the narrow railway bridge. The tennis courts, paddling pool and children's playground were some of the facilities in the park in 1938. Between the trees on the left is the tower of St Charles' church and on the far right is the spire of St Andrew's.

Members of Hadfield Tennis Club played on the park courts throughout the 1930s and '40s. Several people are wearing spectacles in the style of the day, knee-length skirts and simple canvas plimsolls. Long before expensive trainers, this footwear was quite adequate even though the shoes needed whitening each time they were worn. Two sisters in the photograph are Marion and Dorothy Derbyshire.

Some members of the tennis club also played for the Hadfield Badminton Club using the courts at the Liberal Club on Bank Street. The length of the lady's skirt on the right would have been considered quite shocking in 1937. They used simple wooden racquets and most of the men would wear long white flannels.

Left: The opening of the water filtration plant on Main Road in Padfield (*c.* 1932) by Alderman George Platt, with Mayor Robert John Boak on the left. On the far right watching the proceedings is a local policeman wearing an old tunic buttoned to the neck. The old police station was on Albert Street in Hadfield.

Below: Workmen with pickaxes on Jones Street in the 1930s. Wearing the usual working clothes of the day they were starting to dig the foundations for the new community hall off Station Road in Hadfield. The buildings at the rear of the terraced houses would be the coal sheds and shared outside toilets.

Watched by local children, the foundations were completed ready for stone footings to be laid before the building work commenced. One little boy got off his three-wheeler to have a closer look. In the background are the Bleaklow hills and houses at Padfield. The building on the left is the old blacksmith's, owned by A. O'Niel.

Mayor John Cuthbert with other dignitaries at the opening ceremony of the community hall in the late 1930s. Wearing a single watch chain, Alderman Richard Sellars (mayor between 1927 and 1928 and again in 1939) is third from the right. The man on the left is sporting a 'Double Albert' watch chain, which was popularised by Prince Albert in the nineteenth century.

The Duke of Kent visited Hadfield in December 1935 and the Hadfield League of Social Services
presented him with this model aircraft. Hadfield Nursery School started in the League's clubroom for the
unemployed in 1937. The foundation stone for their new school was laid in 1938 and was built by the
unemployed.

The American-born Lady Astor opened the new nursery school in June 1939. Alderman Richard
Sellars was the mayor and Alderman Ernest Haigh was chairman of the governors. The League of Social
Services handed over the running of the school to the local education authority in 1941, and Mrs Laurie
handed over a history of the school to the mayor.

Right: Mrs Laurie, the pioneer of Hadfield's League of Social Services charity in the 1920s, accompanies the first female Member of Parliament Lady Nancy Astor (1879-1964), left, at the school's opening ceremony. As her personal gift, Lady Astor had offered the salary of a superintendent if the League would build a proper nursery school in Hadfield.

Below: Mersey Bank House, situated between The Carriage Drive and Chapel Lane, was the home of the mill-owning families. In the 1930s Mr Ernest Wilman from Station Mills resided there. This gathering took place in the 1930s, and local families are watching over the fence. The home is now a residence for the elderly.

A police officer near Mersey Bank House on a winter's day at the turn of the twentieth century. In 1907 John Platt and Edward Platt JP lived there. Their name lives on in Platt Street, Padfield. The house was built in around 1855. To the left is St Charles' Roman Catholic church.

St Charles Borromeo church was built by the first Baron Howard of Glossop, Lord Edward Fitzalan Howard, and opened in 1858. A school with only one classroom was built in the same year and extended in 1880. St Joseph's convent was built in the church grounds in 1887 for the Sisters of Charity, who stayed until 1977.

The first trams ran from old Glossop to the Palatine on Station Road in 1903; a journey cost two old pennies. There was also a loop line to Whitfield owned by the Urban Electricity Supply Company, and 20,000 passengers were using local trams each week by 1904.

This Glossop wagon was involved in an accident on the corner of Salisbury Street and Station Road. The building on the right later became a bank. Streets were lit with oil lamps from 1842, but it wasn't until 1861 that gas lamps began to light the streets. The trams stopped in 1927 after the first motor buses had been introduced in 1926.

The Ashton-under-Lyne Amateur Radio Society visited Hadfield enthusiast Mr Joe Moore (2FXW, back right) in 1934. Joe lived on Bank Street and was the manager of Hadfield Picturedrome at the top of the same street, near to Wesley Street, from 1925. Previously he had been the assistant projectionist at the Theatre Royal on Victoria Street in Glossop from the age of eleven. His son, Donald Joseph Clement Moore, was a boyhood friend of television personality Stuart Hall, whose father ran a baker's shop at 52 Station Road in Hadfield. The Picturedrome was all on one floor except for an alcove that housed a dozen seats, the preserve of VIPs, Donald and his mates!

Other members of the radio society included Cecil Noakes (3DFX), Harry Lapworth, Barrie Simpson (2HAP), Bill Green, Harry Buxton (2AJP), Norman Brown, Jack Partington (3PY), Basil Smith and Romas Shing. Long before Citizens Band Radio, members would contact each other using their radio call signs (the numbers and letters indicated in brackets). With a radio set costing £7 in 1937, it was an expensive hobby. Some of the group learnt how to make their own equipment with the vast stores of valves, speakers and dials that cluttered up their homes.

The Glossop and District Radio Society held their meetings in the Picturedrome on Bank Street. The building originally opened as the Hippodrome cinema in the early years of the twentieth century. Some of the members included John Ginever, Joe Moore, Roy Sherlock, Sam Torkington, Messrs Sidebottom and Morris and Sam Ratcliffe.

The Radio Society often went on field trips to test the reception on their equipment. High places such as Hartshead Pike near Ashton and Werneth Low in Hyde were popular venues. Here in 1937 the group seems to have chosen a grassy area in front of a collapsed stone wall. Their call sign G3PY is displayed on the central receiver.

St Andrew's church had a mission hall on Lees Street in Woolley Bridge. Younger members of the congregation put on a play that was held in the schoolroom of Brookfield chapel. Perhaps the photograph was taken before the performance and the serious faces reflected some nervousness about remembering their lines!

There was a slump in the cotton industry in the early 1920s, when overseas trade was lost. This affected the availability of work locally. In Hadfield sixty-seven per cent of men were unemployed in 1933 and it was deemed the second most depressed area in the country. A Christmas party was held locally for the unemployed and their families in 1934.

The Methodist church on Station Road was used as an extra classroom for children born at the end of the war – 'the baby boomers' born in 'the bulge year'. Scholars from St Andrew's had to walk each day to the chapel until extra classrooms were built in the 1950s. The church later became the Carmel Christian Centre.

A flash of lightning, photographed from Bank Street in Hadfield looking towards Mottram in September 1934. For photographic enthusiasts, the exposure was one fifth of a second, taken on a three and a half by seven and a half-inch glass plate camera.

Above: Winters were often quite severe; icicles hang from the church gutters and snow has drifted over the surrounding walls making Stanyforth Street a no-driving zone. These schoolboys, out shopping for their mother, seemed to be enjoying it. The trees in the church grounds used to attract owls and after dark their hooting could be heard in nearby streets.

Left: Mr William Newby (aged seventy-two) set off from Hadfield in September 1939 to visit his son in Kilburn, London, a distance of 203 miles, with only a parcel tied to the handlebars, a bag, possibly his gas mask on his back, string for bicycle clips and wearing sandals. We don't know if he arrived safely!

Landlady Mrs Torkington with her collection of medals, brass and copper wares at the Arundel Arms on Cemetery Road in 1939. Because of its close proximity to the graveyards, the public house (built in 1828) was known as 'The Deadmans'. It closed in around 1957 and then opened as a kennels and cattery until 1994.

A wedding from the 1920s. Fashions of the day included spats on the groom's shoes, a three-piece suit with the waistcoat sporting a Double Albert chain for his fob watch and a shirt with a flyaway collar. The bride wears a cloche hat, pearls, a short tiered dress, gloves and lisle stockings.

Left: This couple from the 1930s, named on the photograph only as Jack and Ethel, seem quite well-to-do, with his frock coat, top hat and gloves, and her long dress with pearl detail at the neck and veil. She carries the traditional large bouquet, making it a 'wreath and veil do.'

Below: At the wedding of Ada Williams the bridesmaids and bride all carried large bouquets. It was also fashionable for the ladies to wear large hats. Living on Park Road, Ada was for many years a teacher at St Andrew's infant school and she became the Mayor of Glossop in 1966, during the borough's centenary year.

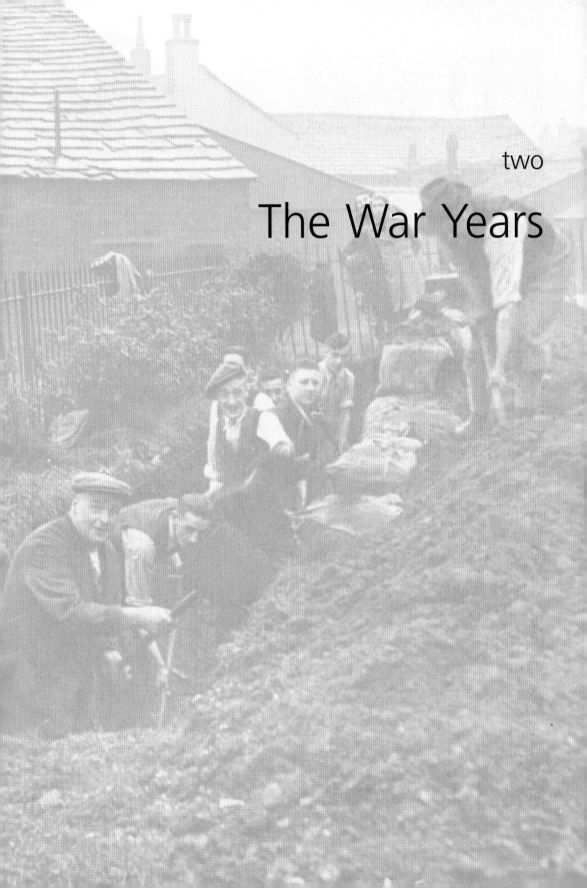

two

The War Years

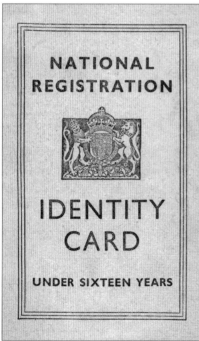

NATIONAL
REGISTRATION

IDENTITY
CARD

UNDER SIXTEEN YEARS

Above: With the Second World War approaching, and watched by a neighbouring family from the top end of Hadfield Road, most of these local men, digging out trenches ready for the arrival of air-raid shelters, managed to smile for the camera. War was declared in September 1939.

Left: Identity cards were issued from 1939 for all residents. Children up to sixteen were issued with a buff-coloured card to be signed by parent, guardian or 'other person having charge or control'. Inside were the words, 'For official entry only. Any other entry or any alterations, marking or erasure is punishable by a fine or imprisonment or both'.

Left: Harry Buxton, leaning against a pile of sandbags, was a warden on air-raid duties and is seen showing schoolchildren where to go in case of an attack. For them it seemed a light-hearted adventure but the faces on most of the adults show rather more apprehension.

Below: When people were encouraged to grow their own produce to survive the war, parks, playing fields and grassy areas were ploughed up to grow vegetables. There were 200 allotments in the Glossop area in 1940. These residents in Bank Street consider 'digging for victory.'

On Roughfields, Mr Gill had turned his allotment shed into a kind of patriotic 'Heath Robinson' shelter. Decked in a straw boater he seems to be working a piece of stone, watched by a younger man smoking his Woodbine. Beyond the greenhouse, wagons from the railway are passing en route for the Woodhead tunnel.

Metal was in short supply and by 1943 all iron railings from houses and public buildings had to be cut down and melted for the war effort. Iron and steel merchants used acetylene torches on the railings in Walker Street, Hadfield, loaded them onto their lorry for transportation. The council refused to part with the gates at Manor Park.

Over 220 ARP Wardens wearing tin helmets with a white letter 'W' and blue overalls were recruited in 1939. It was their job to supervise air raid procedures in the streets and shelters, to issue gas masks and check the blackout. A. Stone, S. Woodward, E. Longson, Mrs Lawton, Mrs Barber, Harry Buxton, Mr Chadwick, Mr Crabtree, W. Foot and Cecil Bowden are among those here in front of the warden's post on Hadfield Cross. Huge piles of sandbags were used to protect important buildings from bomb damage. Windows were blacked out, street lighting was switched off and over 18,000 ration books were issued; people kept buckets of sand and water to use with stirrup pumps to extinguish fires. Air raid sirens costing around forty pounds were placed on roofs. By 1940 the Home Guard and an auxiliary fire service were formed, place names and signposts were obliterated and church bells were silenced. Men registered to join the armed forces at recruitment centres and by 1942 there was also conscription of female workers. Petrol, soap, clothes and other non-food commodities were also rationed. Utility fashions and home-made clothes became the order of the day. There were restrictions on coal and some people began secret stores inside their homes so their outdoor coal sheds would seem empty. By 1943 it was compulsory for all women between the ages of 18 and 45 to work part-time. The Post Office began to issue pre-stamped aerogrammes for forces mail. By 1944 a partial 'dim-out' replaced the blackout.

Above: The Red Cross Society met in the library in 1940 to knit blankets. The Revd White always opened the meetings with a prayer and then helped to pack the goods. Even though a sign on the back wall requested silence the women had a singsong whilst they worked and also organised whist and beetle drives to swell the funds.

Left: Sergeant Douglas Henshall and war reserve Harry Buxton were two members of the Glossop borough police force during the war. During each shift, the sergeant regularly met with his officers to check and sign pocket books at certain points on their beat. This check was made at the top of Station Road in 1942.

Opposite below: Boys from Castle secondary modern school had a break from their lessons to learn how to wear their gas masks. In a radio broadcast in 1939 mothers were encouraged to put on their masks and call it 'mummy's funny face' so their children would not be terrified by the apparition if it had to be used for real.

Evacuees arrived from Manchester and Lowestoft at Glossop Station in June 1940. Mr C. Lord was the chief billeting officer who sent children to various places by bus. Two hundred working-class children were received in Hadfield by school headmasters Mr Booth and Mr Bowden and by the Revd White. Over 1,000 children stayed in local homes and attended local schools.

Left: 17,500 gas masks were issued in 1938, one for everyone in Glossop, because of the threat of gas attacks by Hitler's Luftwaffe. This boy treated his as yet another toy. Much younger children were given blue and red masks that looked like Mickey Mouse and babies were enclosed in a complete suit.

Below: During February 1940 heavy snow fell on the railway lines and troops were engaged in clearing the tracks. They consisted of Polish refugees, German prisoners of war and the Pioneer Corps. It was essential that the Woodhead rail links were kept open to get coal from Yorkshire for vital manufacturing processes.

The heavy snowfall of 1940 closed many schools. Neighbours helped each other to dig through the drifting snow that sometimes reached up to the bedroom windows. With only open coal fires to heat houses, it was common to have frost on the inside of the windows, and most houses had outdoor toilets where the pipes burst in frosty weather, making them unusable.

Not many homes had bathrooms in the 1940s so most mothers bathed their children in the tin bath in front of a roaring fire using hot water from kettles and pans. Each winter even indoor pipes often froze and burst. Thick clothing and warm food were the way to survival.

Left: Despite the rationing and shortage of commodities, couples still married and did the best they could to make their day special. Wedding cakes were often made from a cardboard shape and then iced and decorated. Brides wore their best dress or costume and this lady also managed to have a veil.

Below: The war in Europe ended in May 1945 (VE Day) and finally peace came in August 1945 (VJ Day). It seemed a long time since the last night of peace. In Hadfield many celebrated by dancing in front of the cenotaph at the top of Station Road, on the smooth area where the trams used to run.

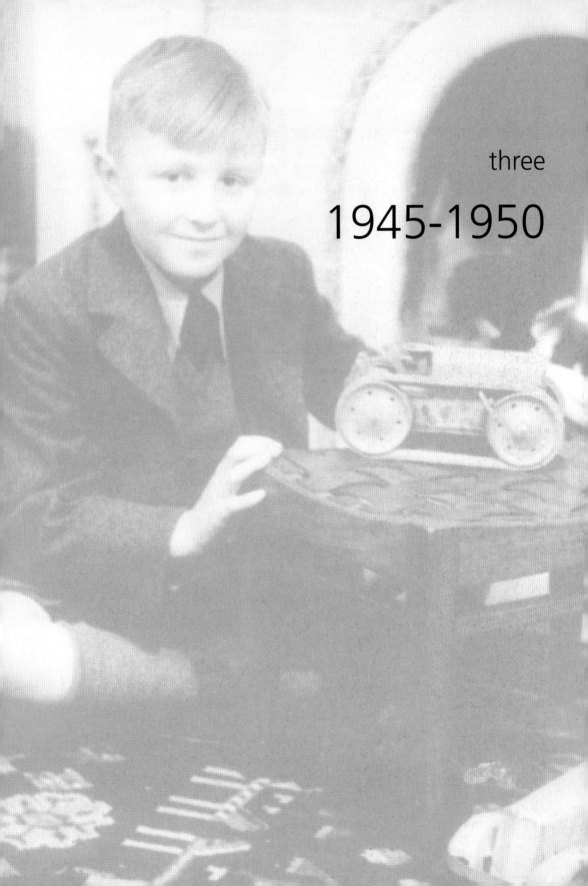

three

1945-1950

Many homes still had the old black grate with integral ovens for cooking. On the left, at the side of the stone sink, there is a gas burner to heat water for wash day. For this boy it was all quite normal and he was happy as long as he had Donald Duck to play with.

This home had a modern tiled fireplace in the sitting room with a 'companion set' to the right to clean the hearth. Often the rooms had a carpet square with lino or bare floorboards around the edge and a rug in front of the fire. This local boy was content to play in the warmth with his tin tractor and car.

The parish church displayed the Union flags, reminding those who entered of the men and women who had given their lives for their country. The words of the hymns and psalms sung at that time no doubt reflected on this price of freedom. The church is now very different, with chairs, fitted carpets and a very welcoming and spacious interior.

There had been many austere weddings during the war years, and although there was still rationing on many items couples saw hope for the future and married as men returned from the war. On the right is the Revd White, who was one of the two clergymen who had officiated at this more lavish wedding.

Houses at Woolley Bridge facing the Spread Eagle Hotel, whose cobbled forecourt is visible on the right. In front of the car is the end of Lees Row, where the St Andrew's mission hall stood. The billboards on the terrace-end display the daily headlines and advertise the contents of the magazine *Home Notes*.

The houses at Woolley Bridge were demolished in the 1940s. Middleton's newsagent, selling the *Evening Chronicle* and the *Daily Despatch*, remained open for many years afterwards. The directional sign to the left of the shop doorway pointed the way on the A57 to Glossop (two and a quarter miles away) and Sheffield (twenty-six miles away).

This Glossop bus, on its way to Tintwistle and Hollingworth, crashed into a lamp standard on Newshaw Lane, Hadfield in November 1945. Tragically, Mary Hoyland (aged fifty-seven) from Glossop was killed and seventeen other passengers were injured by flying glass. Nearby council houses were built from natural stone by Glossop Corporation in 1919.

The white house near the cross on Hadfield Road was originally a farmhouse. The farmer used to drive his cattle to graze on fields now occupied by houses on Higher Barn Road. On the reconstructed garden wall is a date stone from 1724, bearing the initials 'WM' or 'WH', from the old farm building, which was rebuilt in September 1946.

The winter of 1947 saw severe blizzards, making it the worst winter on record. Padfield was one of the worst areas for drifting snow; in some streets it reached the height of the bedroom windows. Traffic came to a standstill, pipes froze and services were cut off.

The area had seen the heaviest snowfall in one day in 1933 when snow started to fall at lunchtime and continued until 10 p.m. Many roads, especially near the cemetery, were again blocked in 1947 with deep snow. This car in North Road had been abandoned by its owners, who later came to dig it out.

An electric radio cost twelve pounds in 1940, but after the war there was plenty of surplus radio equipment for sale from the Admiralty. Radio Society members eagerly added to their collection to further their hobby of communicating with fellow enthusiasts around the region. With modern technology this wall of dials and speakers could now be condensed into one small box!

The Revd J.H. Roe from Ashton and the Revd H.J. Watson from Manchester dressed as John and Charles Wesley in 1948. They rode from Padfield Methodist church to Bank Street chapel addressing the crowds at the station and at Lambgates. The pageantry preceded the opening of an exhibition to mark the first anniversary of the Revd Martland's ministry at the Hadfield chapel.

Shell Mex petrol was on sale at Lawton's garage on Station Road. This was the only place where Hadfield and Padfield residents could get a taxi. The garage owner showed off his new coach at the corner of Lambgates. It had a seating capacity of twenty-eight and a top speed of 25 mph.

After the war many women continued to work as 'clippies' on the local bus service. The drivers and conductors had time for a break at the terminus in front of the cenotaph on Station Road before the next journey to Glossop. The rounded building on the left is the District Bank at the corner of Salisbury Street.

The St Andrew's mission fancy dress party was organised by the Mothers Union in around 1950. Mill owner Henry Lees allowed workers to use a house next to his Woolley Bridge Mill on Lees Road as a Christian meeting room. It closed after 100 years of fellowship in November 1964 with a social that included a film show and sing song.

The Revd J. Rawlinson, Bishop of Derby, dedicated the Mother's Memorial Chapel at St Andrew's in October 1948. The Mothers Union organisation had reached its jubilee in 1943 and members raised £300 to transform this corner of the church into a chapel. Today the MU has over 3 million members in seventy-one countries.

Left: Cameras and photographic equipment have advanced greatly since this picture was taken in 1948. The camera used large glass plates, which were carried in the leather bag. Joseph Nicephore Niepce took the first photograph in 1826 and Louis Jacques Mande Daguerre created the first image on glass plates. William Henry Fox Talbot was responsible for the first photographs in England.

Below: Hadfield's identical twins, Kenneth (on the left) and Derrick Turner, in 1949. They were back home on leave from the RAF's Pershore training camp in Worcestershire. Were the differing buttons on their caps their only distinguishing feature?

The original entrance to Chapel Lane started across Hadfield Road at the end of Walker Street and was so named because John Thornley built a Methodist chapel in 1804 lower down the lane. To the right there were farmer's fields with stiles dividing grazing animals from the cornfields, accessible through a path near to Hadfield Cross.

The meadows off Chapel Lane, which were rich in wild flowers in the 1950s, were a wonderful place for local children to discover nature and wildlife. The paths led past Mersey Bank House near to St Charles' church and continued down to Woolley Bridge Road. Twelve years after this photograph was taken, houses were built on the land.

After the war, Harry Buxton left his position as a police photographer to resume general photography, working from his home in Walker Street. The front room was used as a studio and the dark room was the room under the stairs. Later he became a freelance photographer for the *Glossop Chronicle* and the *High Peak Reporter* until 1967.

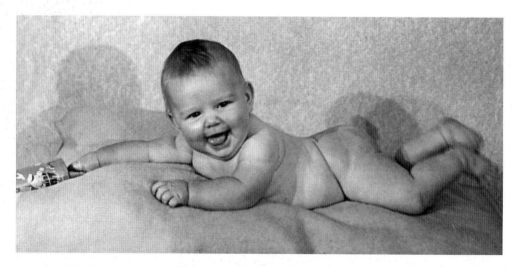

Mr & Mrs Wood's baby (from Shaw Lane in Hadfield) was the subject of just one of the many happy baby and child portraits taken at Walker Street. Clutching a rattle and enjoying freedom from a nappy, you can almost hear him chuckling.

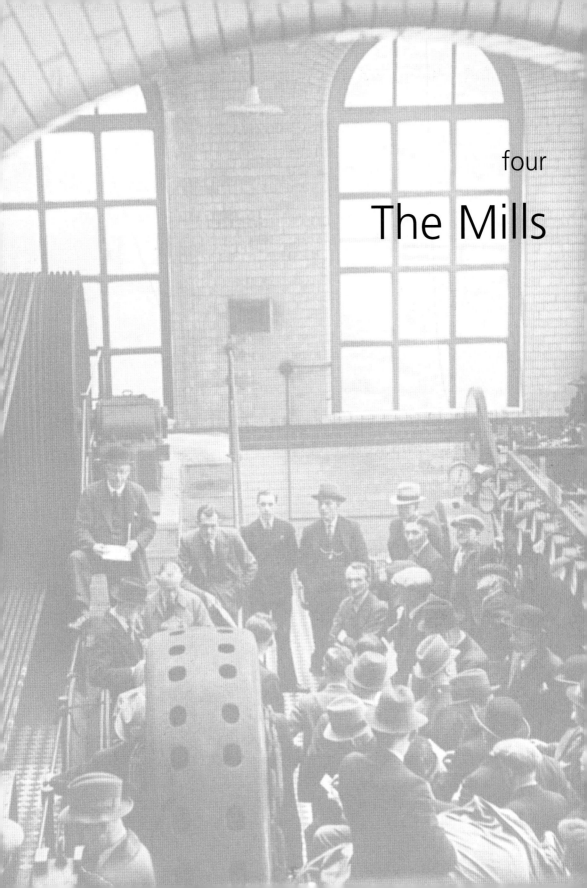

four

The Mills

The mills in Glossopdale first started in the eighteenth century and by 1880 the area was very important in the cotton industry. Many households already had people who could spin and weave wool and these skills were used and adapted to form the workforce of the early mills. Local men who had amassed enough money built the first cotton-spinning mills and became a new class of mill owners, with great power and influence in the development and running of the area. Amongst them were John and Thomas Thornley, William Barber, Robert Lees, William Platt, James Braddock and Thomas and William Shepley Rhodes. The sides of the River Etherow and Padfield Brook were ideal locations for the mills to use the power of water to drive the machinery. On the River Etherow were Bottom Mill and Vale House Mill, the Mersey Mills, Dalton's printworks, Garden Mill and Bridge Mill (also known as Waterside Mill and Sidebottom's Mill). On Padfield Brook were Brookside, Thornley, Hadfield Lodge, Rhodes Top Mill, Mouse Nest Mill, Padfield Brook and Station Mill (also known as Platt Mill).

James Hargreaves from Lancashire was the inventor of the spinning jenny in 1764. It enabled one person to spin several threads instead of the single thread given by the old spinning wheel. It was fed with strands of cotton fibre wound on bobbins. It pulled the strands out thinner, twisted them and wound the threads on bobbins.

Opposite above: Padfield Methodist chapel at the top of Post Street. The primary school on Rhodes Street led on to Main Road with Oldham's (the milkman), Brierley's farm, Whitehouse farm, the old Liberal Club and Cross farm. To the right is the Independent chapel on Temple Street. Above the millpond were allotments and Rhodes Top Mill, below the Bleaklow hills.

Opposite below: Padfield Brook mill was demolished in September 1961 after many years of disuse. It was built in 1793 by Robert Lees and known as Little Mill. Lees originally came from Alt Hill near Oldham to build the rushcart for the Wakes festival. He married Sarah Baker, a local cotton manufacturer's daughter, and built Brook House and cottages known as Lees Row.

Rhodes Top Mill, seen here with Padfield Brook in the foreground, was built in around 1780 as a cotton mill on Platt Street. It incorporated Braddock's, Clarke's and Lower mills into its complex in 1874 and became known as Hadfield Mills. In 1930 floods caused the floor to collapse in the weaving shed and looms piled onto each other.

An auction of the old machinery marked the end of manufacturing of Rhodes Top Mill in around 1947. The sombre faces of those present showed the sadness felt locally as this cotton mill closed. During the war the mill was also used to store food for rationing. Boxes of provisions were unloaded under the cover of darkness so the public would not see them.

J. Kershaw of Bolton used part of the complex of the mills on Padfield Brook as a tannery from 1921 until around 1947. It was demolished in October 1951; a secret tunnel that was thought to lead to the other mills was hunted for but never found. In the background under the roof trusses is Rhodes Top Mill.

The top two storeys of Rhodes Top Mill were taken down in December 1961. From 1874 until 1914 the premises were used to store materials for Station Mill. In 1929 it became Wilman's, manufacturers of silk noils for furnishings. At the lower end of Platt Street in Padfield, the coal-laden railway wagons head for Hadfield railway station.

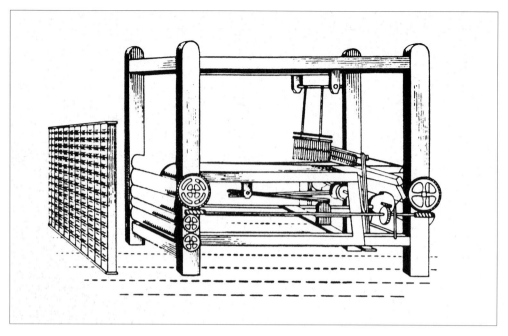

Edmund Cartwright (1743-1823) invented the first water-powered loom in 1785. It was possible on this machine to interweave the warp and weft threads of cotton, as a hand weaver had done by passing a shuttle in and out. He also invented a machine for combing wool and another for making rope.

An early photograph of Rhodes Bottom Mill at Woolley Bridge, with the hills of the Longdendale Valley in the background. Later it was known as the Mersey Mills, and then it became part of a group of buildings known as The Combine.

Some of the workers at Ferrostatics, with tool-making equipment. Ferrostatics started an engineering works (making tools, jigs and gauges) in the 1940s at Bottom Mill before moving to their High Street East works in Glossop.

On the left the tower of the River Etherow Bleaching Company peeps over the rooftops of the Mersey Mills complex at Woolley Bridge, known locally as The Combine. The railway line ran across the road and onto sidings near Gamesley for trains that brought raw materials to Waterside Mill and then collected the finished products for relocation.

Firemen hosing down after a fire at The Combine complex at Woolley Bridge, with locals looking on through the window frame. Severe damage was caused to part of the building. The Combine incorporated the site of Bottom Mill and the Mersey Mills.

Demolition workers precariously perched on the edges of the Mersey Mills at Woolley Bridge. Armed only with a metal crowbar, each stone of the factory wall was knocked off in turn, and those below had to look up to be warned of the danger of men working above.

A policeman chats to the foreman as the Mersey Mills were demolished, and a handcart is loaded with timber as the workmen reach ground level. Other workers using a ladder had started to demolish the roof of the building on the left, revealing the top of the River Etherow Bleaching Company's clock tower.

Situated next to the River Etherow, this area has always been prone to flooding. After heavy rain in December 1965, the Etherow Bleach Works, John Walton's and Hadfield Silks were all flooded, along with many houses and the Co-operative store. Walton's textile works came to Woolley Bridge in 1957 and printed fabric and Tootal ties.

Waterside Mill was a huge complex of mills built in the late 1700s on the River Etherow. In 1795 there were three buildings on the site known as Turner's factory. In 1819 there was a four-storey building known as Garden Mill, and in 1855 Bridge Mills became part of the complex. In 1977 the chimney was reduced in height.

During the celebrations for the Coronation of King George VI and Queen Elizabeth in 1937, the workforce of Waterside Mill were allowed time to dress up and wave their flags. Streamers in patriotic colours were draped between the looms and a picture of the future queen can be seen on the left. Usually the working day was from 7.30 a.m. to 5.30 p.m.

Maconochies came to Waterside in 1940 after their Millwall plant was damaged in The Blitz. At Hadfield workers packed canned meat, vegetables and fruit to supply the demand for food during the Second World War. Scott took Maconochies puddings on his ill-fated expedition to the Antarctic in 1912 and a tin was found forty years later at one of his food dumps.

A party was held in Maconochies' canteen to celebrate VE Day in 1945, with 370 people attending. The factory was famous for producing Pan-yan Pickles and Kep Sauce and due to a shortage of workers women from other countries were invited to work here after the war. Later Maconochies became Whitesides, then Rowntrees in 1959, and finally Nestlé and Premier Foods until 2003.

The Bleacher's Association were the last residents of the old mill at Waterside before it was demolished in 1953. During the war it had been used as a munitions store, and this inscription with a picture of ducks and a heart was found carved on a stone windowsill. It probably meant that Jepson, the stone mason, had signed a pledge to be teetotal in 1847.

Waterside Mill, which once employed thousands of people, closed in 1976 after 200 years of continuous activity in textiles. A large part of the site was demolished in 1977. Glossop Heritage Centre has displays including looms used in the cotton industry and illustrated embroidery to remind us of the days of cotton mills in Glossopdale.

five

1951-1955

Left: In the 1950s professional photographers were encumbered with heavy equipment. This early flash gun was made from a torch and a metal dish, and similar ones were used until the invention of the electronic flash gun.

Below: Sashalite photoflash bulbs were the size of modern day electric light bulbs. A new bulb had to be used for every indoor photograph, which necessitated the carrying of a large box to accommodate them. Once used they became very hot and resembled a clouded silvery mass inside the glass.

The River Etherow at Woolley Bridge marks the boundary between Cheshire and Derbyshire. The road bridge was built in around 1821. Workmen and local schoolboys watched as the metal support was lowered into position ready for a new wooden footbridge in February 1951. The building on the left was the old toll house, and at the time of this photograph it was a sweet shop.

Padfield's independent pantomime in 1952. From left to right, back row: Muriel Walker, Alwin Senior, Alice Higginbottom, Mary Gunner, Mavis and Mary Barnes, Lilian Turner, Joan Basford, Geoff Scarratt. Middle row: Eric Wilde, Grace Laite, Frank Wilde, Fred Hulme, Gwyneth Hughes, Doreen Harris, Jim Hodson, Kenneth Wilde, John Higginbottom, Doreen Brocklehurst, Elsie Cheal. Young girls, standing: Eileen Wilde, Christine Walpole, Jean Wilde, Eileen Brocklehurst. Front row: Peter Cordy, Graham Thomson, David Harris and Jim Higginbottom.

Some of the children in Mrs Furlong's class at St Andrew's school in 1952 were Joyce Mitchell, Marjorie Dean, Christine Bray, Elaine Bentley, Kathryn Sheldon, Leonard Oliver, Alan Sutton, Leonard Harrison, Jim Stead, Julian Davies, Ken Hatton, Tony Leah, Barrie Oldham, John Pass, Glenys Morris, Janet Mottram, Keith Scott, Kenneth Rice and Mary Povey.

St Andrew's school, built in 1855, held a two-day floral bazaar in November 1953 and raised £2,000 to refurbish the Railway Street school and the church. From the left are the Revd A.C.M. White, Pamela Stanley, the Duke of Devonshire, Joyce Mitchell, Major Cochrane, Margaret Buxton and school headmaster Mr Bowden. The three girls presented buttonholes to the platform party.

Mr John Pennington and his son cutting hay at Walton's farm off Dinting Road. In the background is the Dinting railway viaduct, which was opened in December 1845, 1,455ft long and standing over 100ft above the water below.

Looking towards Dinting Viaduct at the junction of Newshaw Lane and Dinting Road on a winter's day in the 1950s. In 1967 the Dinting Railway Centre was opened in the former Great Central engine shed, to the left of the viaduct. It was known as the Bahamas Locomotive Society and formed to secure the LMS Jubilee class 4-6-0 No. 5596 *Bahamas* for preservation.

Above: Looking towards Padfield from Redgate in the winter of 1952. The name of the latter is thought to have derived from the time of a great battle that took place between a Saxon chief called Alman and the so-called Prince of Mouselow, whose camp occupied the opposing hill, Melandra, the site of a former Roman hill fort. There was much blood shed during the battle which is said to have run down the hill. The place where Alman died became known as Alman's Heath.

Left: Dressed in his waistcoat, watch-chain and flat cap, Mr Jim Harrison was a crown green bowler at the Hadfield club, near the chapel on Bank Street. In July 1952 he celebrated fifty years of bowling.

Mr Noel Oliver (of Dinting Road) showed off his car to a friend on Walker Street in Hadfield. The 30hp petrol engine (inset) had been converted to diesel in August 1952. The top speed was 70mph and he had done over 400 miles since its conversion, but he could only get the fuel some miles away in Hyde.

Also seen on Walker Street in December 1953 was the new Corporation dust cart, the back compartment of which could tilt at ninety degrees to allow rubbish to be shaken down, allowing the maximum amount possible to be collected in one journey. Each week dustmen carried all household refuse in metal bins to and fro between back gardens and the cart.

Hadfield library was the gift of local mill owner Edward Platt in 1905. It was illuminated to mark the Coronation of Queen Elizabeth II in 1953. To commemorate this special time there were street parties, houses were decorated with flags and streamers in national colours and bonfires were lit. Children received engraved glass mugs and sweet tins from their schools.

Left: The Waterside infant school, which had been closed for many years, was demolished in July 1953. It opened in 1872 and was the first Church of England school in Hadfield. It had 150 pupils in the late 1800s, from the Waterside and Brosscroft areas.

Opposite below: St Andrew's in 1954. From left to right, back row: D. Rhodes, D. Bailey, S. Harrison, K. Ridyard, B. Sharp, T. Mellor, J. Sheldon, J. Gunner, Mrs Booth, C. Betts, B. Sidebottom, Y. Jones, A. Boak, S. Byrom, ? Barnes, E. Gent, J. Frazer, Mr Bowden, R. Wilson, J. Grantham, N. Walton, A. Mills, S. Buxton, G. Harrison, J. Greensmith, -?-, -?-, K. Renshaw, -?-, S. Towers, M. Higginbottom, C. Bayley, -?-, I. Rogerson, J. Gerrard, M. Buxton, B. Slack, B. Goodyear, F. Ninnes, A. McVey, J. Bintcliffe, N. Carhart, F. Morris.

St Andrew's in 1953. From left to right, back row: B. Hadfield, M. Gibbs, N. Wood, T. Gunner, K. Hurst, P. Bramhall, B. Williams, G. Chapman, Mrs Joan Booth, G. Barnes, D. Mills, A. Rowell, D. Scott, A. Hill, K. Heppinstall, M. Race, R. Ibbotson, S. Lawton, S. Clarke, B. Sharp, E. Platt, M. Ackley, J. Robinson, S. Jones, J. Barber, M. Bunting, B. Thompson, G. Johnson, A. Wright, F. Ackley, M. Taylor, J. Calverly.

Above: At Castle school sports day in around 1955, headmaster Mr Fred Booth presented the winning trophies to members of Shaftsbury House, John Parks and Tommy Gunner (left) and June Kay and Alan Hill (right). The school was established in 1930 and with West End secondary modern it become Glossop's comprehensive school in 1965. A new comprehensive school opened in Hadfield in 1971.

Right: The Revd White was the curate at St Andrew's church from 1911 to 1917. He became the vicar after the death of the Revd J. Hadfield and remained in the position until his own death, aged 76, in 1955. This bookmark shows early pictures of the church, the badge of the church's Lads Brigade, the brigade hymn and the Revd White when he was the rural dean.

six

1956-1960

Above: Wearing their regulation aprons, these pupils in the woodwork room at Castle school in around 1955 were taught by Mr Ingham. From left to right they were Alan Hill, Jim Higginbottom, Graham Brocklehurst, David Moss, -?-, George Rhodes, John Gunner and Jim Bintcliffe. It was an era when girls did cookery and needlework, whilst the boys made various things from wood and metal.

Left: The Revd John Ernest Fredrick Styles MA was inducted as vicar in July 1956 at Hadfield parish church. He was very interested in choral music and worked with the church choir until he left the parish in March 1960.

The increased number of births after the Second World War meant that local schools soon became very overcrowded. Some children had to walk to other venues to take their lessons until two new classrooms were constructed on the playing fields behind Castle Secondary School. Work began in February 1956 and classes moved in at the start of the new term in September of that year.

Inside one of the new classrooms at St Andrew's school in 1956. Some of Standard 4 class seen with headmaster Mr C. Bowden, including Christine White, Kathleen Straw, Barbara Shaw, Mary Povey, Leonard Harrison, Kathryn Sheldon, Celia Groves, Joyce Mitchell, Beryl Dean, Murial Milner, Leonard Oliver, Colin Fielding, Albert Stevenson and Arthur Rice.

Looking up Redgate from the area known as Little Padfield in 1957, with Castle Hill in the background surrounded by trees. Also known as Mouselow, this hill was originally a stronghold for the ancient Britons. The Romans drove them out and razed the motte and bailey castle, which had been built by William de Peverel, to the ground.

Above: It was decided that the redundant wartime air raid shelters in the playground of the old St Andrew's school should come down. The school gates opened on to Railway Street. The sign for Earles Cement over the shelter roofs was on the building suppliers at the corner of Park Road.

Right: For years the shelters had been forbidden territory at playtimes but of course children sneaked in when the teacher wasn't looking. Children would pretend they were haunted by 'bogeymen' and dare each other to go inside. At a time when there was no official school uniform, woollen socks (which were often hand knitted), duffel coats and bonnets were the norm.

The area in front of the library was altered in May 1957. New walls were built around the war memorial and the gardens were improved. The seats proved very popular with those waiting for buses, as well as tired shoppers. Some of the shops on Station Road have white cloth sides on their sun blinds.

Morris men in 1958 on Queen Street, with the seventeenth-century Ivy Cottage behind. Before it was a private dwelling the building was used as a convent and a doctor's surgery. To the right is Sparrow Park, a small green area with seating that was once the site of three-storey stone houses with outdoor steps to the top floor.

Even the snowplough had to be dug out on Hadfield Road in the winter of 1958/59. The old lamp on the left was later removed when the area around Hadfield Cross was modernised. The single-storey building behind was Dewsnap's butchers shop and the building with the pointed roof just visible behind the plough was the doctor's surgery.

Like most of the side streets, Walker Street was only accessible on foot in the deep snow. Before the entrance off Hadfield Road was widened, no vehicles could travel along it. It remained a cobbled street until the end of the 1960s. To the right are the Spinners Arms and the trees of Sparrow Park.

The entrance to Chapel Lane was opposite Walker Street. It led down to a Methodist chapel built by mill owner John Thornley at a cost of £200. After the chapel was demolished the graveyard remained behind the walled enclosure to the left. In the distance are buildings on Mersey Bank Road and the hills of Longdendale.

Old Hall on Hadfield Cross dates from 1646 and was built by a family called Hadfield. Opposite there used to be some cottages (built in 1785) and a farm owned by the Dewsnap family. A cross once stood here and the area was regarded as the centre of the village, around which most of the population would have lived.

The ladies of Woolley Bridge mission at rooms on Lees Row in 1959. They were celebrating the eightieth birthday of one of their members, Mrs Elizabeth Rhodes Buxton, seen here seated with flowers and gifts. Amongst those in attendance were Elizabeth's daughter-in-law Janey and granddaughter Margaret, and Mrs Beatrice Shaw with her daughter Freda and sisters Beatrice, Sybil and Muriel Woodward.

In February 1959 the houses next to the Spread Eagle at Woolley Bridge were demolished to make room for a larger car park. The sweet shop on the right was originally a tollhouse at the point where the River Etherow marks the border between Cheshire and Derbyshire. Hadfield people had to walk to the bus shelter to get a bus to Hyde or Ashton.

Above: The houses and former chemist's shop at the corner of Albert Street and Station Road were demolished in May 1960. It is now a car park opposite the Willow Bank elderly persons home, built in red brick and the former dwelling of the Patchett family, who owned a local butchers.

Left: The Revd J. McCoy was the vicar at St Andrew's church from September 1960. He worked with local teenagers, providing a youth club and taking them on rambles. He left for Ireland in August 1963 to take up a parish in his homeland.

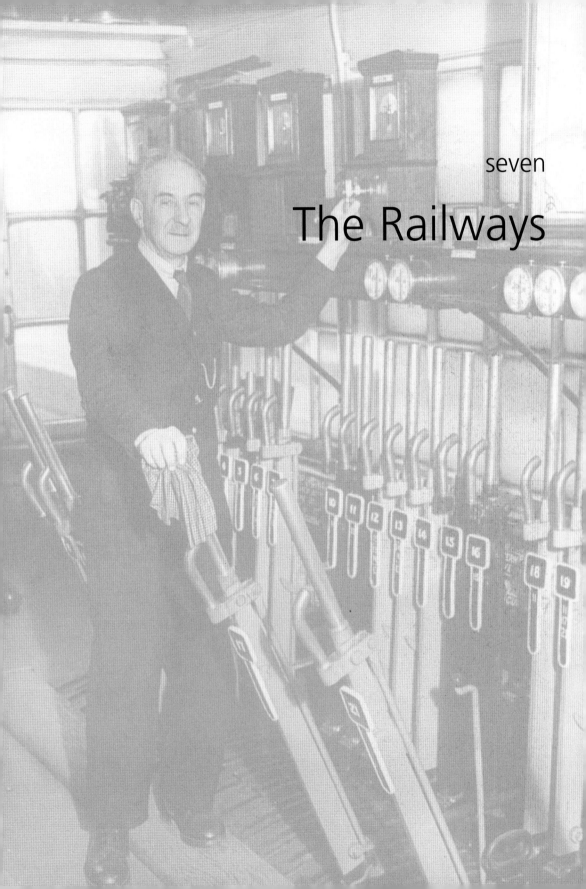

seven

The Railways

Hadfield Station was awarded third prize in the best-kept station competition in August 1952. Stationmaster Mr Bairstow and porters Frank Golvin (centre) and Charlie Dryland, seen here knee deep in blooms, had all contributed to the colourful display. Four years later it was voted the tidiest station and a plaque was awarded in July 1957. Steam trains travelled the line at this time.

Left: The platform and west signal box at Hadfield Railway Station. Mr H. Tongue of Hadfield Road was the porter in 1956 and used his artistic skills to advertise trips to Blackpool, Yarmouth, Cleethorpes, Bridlington, Llandudno and other places that were popular with holidaymakers during Wakes Week holidays, when the mills, factories and many shops all closed.

Opposite below: A steam freight train approaching the station in winter would have unloaded its cargo at Mottram Junction before heading back to Yorkshire via the Woodhead railway tunnel to pick up another load of coal, which was bound for the Manchester area. The stone houses in the background, blackened from years of coal fires and smoke, are on South Marlow Street.

A young enthusiast at Hadfield station in the early 1950s looks on at one of the last steam trains (Number 64304) to run on what was part of the Great Central Railway from Manchester. On the left-hand platform, which was accessible via the footbridge, ladies still had a separate waiting room where the station staff lit a welcoming coal fire.

Diesel-electric locomotives took over from the old steam engines (affectionately known as the 'Puffing Billies') as the line became electrified in 1954. There were engines known as 'Shunters', 'Co-Cos' and 'Bo-Bos'. The Bo-Bo (EM1) were mainly freight trains with eight wheels. The Co-Co (EM2) were mainly passenger trains with twelve wheels.

This express train from Manchester stopped for passengers at Hadfield before continuing its journey up the Longdendale Valley, passing through the new Woodhead tunnel on its way to Penistone and Sheffield in 1958. The houses to the right are on Marlow Street.

Above: The EM2 27000 as it approached Hadfield, travelling on the new fully-electrified line in 1954. The EM1 locomotive (26000, known as 'Tommy') ran on the Netherlands' railways from 1947. The 26020, built at Gorton in 1951, was exhibited at the Festival of Britain and was the first official train to run through the new tunnel at Woodhead.

Left: Hadfield's west signal box was closed in 1964 after 100 years of service. During that time many men had operated the manual levers, read the dials and tapped out messages to colleagues in other boxes to ensure the safe running of passing trains.

Opposite above: There was a two-mile branch line from Dinting to Waterside that served the needs of early mills and factories along its route. The track crossed the road near to the factory at Woolley Bridge where in 1952 John Walton completed new premises for the pre-shrinking, crease resisting and non-felting of Tootal fabrics, and where Pyramid handkerchiefs were made extra-absorbent.

Left: Mr Tom Rowbottom (from Tintwistle) was one of the many signalmen who worked in the signal boxes on the line from Hadfield to Woodhead. The mop is evidence that even in the signal box, staff took pride in keeping everything clean and tidy.

Below: As the new semi-automated signal boxes came into operation, all staff members were trained to use the new instruments to check the progress of the trains on an illuminated tracking system. In a rare sighting in front of a camera, photographer Harry Buxton was always on hand to record new events.

There was a huge rubber dump by the side of the railway track off Woolley Bridge Road in the 1940s, and Glossop Council feared it would catch fire. Residents feared it would encourage vermin and were also concerned that the proposals to raise the level of the land would cause flooding to their homes.

It was the Manchester, Sheffield & Lincolnshire Railway Company that opened the branch line in 1879 to transport goods to and from the mills at Waterside, the Bridge Mills, Mersey Mills and the River Etherow bleach mills. Every year around 15,000 tons of coal and 6,000 tons of paper, fibre, packing materials, fruit and vegetables, pulp, preserves, glassware, cloth, chemicals and rubber were transported.

The last freight train on this route, 69353, completed its final journey in June 1951. Opening the gates to cross Woolley Bridge Road was guard Jim Plant and shunter William Hall. Pedestrians used the wooden footbridge when the trains were crossing the road.

The line closed in 1964, the wooden footbridge came down in January 1966 and the track was removed in 1968, but the gates remained. Hadfield Trades Council wanted them removed to allow for a new footpath, so as to make the route safer for pedestrians.

After travelling through Woolley Bridge the line continued through picturesque scenery to Gamesley and on to the goods yard at Mottram Junction. The driver of the last train on the line (seen here with fireman Mr Robinson) was Bert Turner, who became the mayor in 1954. The guard Jim Plant and shunter William Hall relax inside the guard's van.

Before the track was lifted the North West Locomotive Club organised a special steam train journey for their members on the single-track route in 1964. The line had been used mainly for freight; the only other passengers had been some mill workers who went on an outing to Blackpool, some forty years earlier.

The enthusiasts' train (80044) took them over the A57 at Melandra Bridge in Brookfield. This area near to the Spring Tavern has been the scene of many floods over the years, and sandbags have often been seen at the doors of these terraced houses.

After the closure of the Waterside line, it was decided to raise the road at this point. However, this made it unsafe for high-level vehicles to travel under the bridge, and the 1886 Melandra Bridge was demolished in March 1966. The A57 was closed and traffic was diverted through Hadfield. In the photograph, a cyclist waits while the last girder is removed.

There were also gates to close off Glossop Road at Gamesley to allow trains to pass. After the line closed the sidings reverted to a natural environment with silver birch, wildflowers and extensive wildlife and in the 1990s there was strong opposition to a proposal to dump waste here.

The sidings at Mottram Junction covered in snow during the 1930s. It was here that freight awaited transportation to destinations along the rail system, including coal to keep the mill boilers working, the raw materials used in the mills and finished products.

This poster, found hidden in some furniture in the 1960s, advertises a trip to London run by the Great Northern Railway in around 1840. On careful inspection it would seem that fast trains were not very reliable!

eight

1961-1965

The houses on Lees Row at Woolley Bridge were just off the main road into Glossop. St Andrew's mission used to hold their services and meetings in an upstairs room in one of them. Here, during the early 1960s, the houses are empty and awaiting demolition.

Manchester City Council wanted to improve the housing for over 140,000 of their residents in Gorton, Miles Platting and Openshaw. They worked with Glossop Council to build an overspill estate in 1962. It brought an end to the delightful meadows that had been a favourite walk for so many. Most of the new tenants paid £2 per week for homes on Etherow Way and Styles Close.

As the new houses around Chapel Lane were constructed, the old graveyard (last used in 1859) and its trees were preserved. Mill owner John Thornley built the Methodist chapel that once stood here for just £200 in 1804. Prior to this time Christian meetings had been held in a room in Valehouse mill, but numbers attending had eventually exceeded the capacity of the room.

A new road was made for the Hadfield overspill estate, near to St Charles Borromeo Roman Catholic church on The Carriage Drive, to connect with John Dalton Street. The wall to the right surrounds Mersey Bank House, which is now a nursing home for the elderly.

St Charles Borromeo church, built by Lord Edward Fitzalan Howard and seen here with the new houses to the right, had celebrated its centenary in 1958. Before any churches were built in the area, Catholics worshipped at Glossop Hall. The Lady chapel was demolished in around 1884 to make way for a family vault for Lord Francis Howard. Lord Edward Howard built the local school in 1858.

Above: Next to a small hardware shop on Hadfield Road is Ivy Cottage, home of the Sisters of Charity (who came to Hadfield in 1861) until they moved to the convent built in the church grounds by John Dalton of Hollingworth in 1887. In 1979 the convent opened as a children's home and in 1986 it became an elderly persons' home.

Opposite below: Children from St Andrew's Sunday school presented a pageant at the church called 'The Christian Flarepath' in 1961. It was not the tradition in Hadfield to have Walks of Witness at Whitsuntide; there was instead a walk around the village every year in May on the anniversary of the Sunday school, followed by a service.

Ivy Cottage became the home of Ken Thompson and Florence Ollerenshaw, seen here on their wedding day in December 1957, with the bride's sister Alice. Father Prendergast from St Peter's Roman Catholic church in Stalybridge officiated. The groom's father Clifford, on the right with his wife Kate, was the caretaker at Castle secondary modern school on Hadfield Road.

Left: Mrs Alice Sykes (*née* Manifold) from Buxton was ninety in February 1962. She worked in local mills from the age of ten until she retired, aged sixty-five. She was one of the passengers on the first tram from Hadfield to Glossop in 1903. The journey ran from the Palatine on Station Road via Woolley Bridge to the Queen's Arms in Glossop and it cost 2d!.

Below: Mr Clarence Bowden, who was the headmaster at St Andrew's in Hadfield, became the new Teacher's President in March 1962 at a meeting in Glossop grammar school. Anyone who attended the school will remember those awful curtains on the stage in the school hall!

Above: Just recently (in 2004) Railway Street was closed for the filming of the television series *The League of Gentlemen*. In the winter of 1963 the filming would have been postponed. The stone terraced houses often got ice on the insides of the windows, pipes froze and burst and families crowded into one room to keep warm around an open fire.

Left: The cult television series has also used many locations in Padfield. The snowdrifts in 1963 happened in exposed areas and in Temple Street they reached the height of the bedroom windows. The poor householders had to do some serious digging! The Temple Inn gave its name to the street and later became the Peel's Arms, named after Sir Robert Peel.

Bank Street chapel opened in 1878 and amalgamated with Woolley Bridge Road Methodist chapel in 1963. The Revd John Platt preached at the last service before the congregation, led by the Revd Hazel Cooke, walked in procession to new premises on Station Road in May 1996, with oldest member Phyllis Harrison cutting the ribbon. The old chapel was destroyed by fire in 1997.

Stuart Hall is a well-known face from television. As a youngster he lived at his parent's bakers shop at 52 Station Road and then for several years in Glossop. He has been called upon many times to appear at local functions. Here he presented the Longdendale Darts League Shield, trophies and medals to the finalists at Hadfield Conservative Club in April 1963.

Left: The Revd Arthur Whittaker was inducted as the new vicar of St Andrew's church in December 1963.

Below: Children from St Andrew's school posed for a memorable Christmas photograph in front of characters from a scene from Cinderella, which had been painted by one of the teachers. Among the staff at the time were headmaster Mr Clarence Bowden, Mrs Furlong, Mrs Peggy Davies and Miss Minnie Robinson.

The church and school had close links; most of the scholars attended Sunday school and also went into church on special days in the church's year. On this occasion in 1964 the Sunday school was celebrating its Christmas party in the former Castle school, which was by this time used as the day school.

The Sunday school nativity play was performed in the church in 1964. With the Revd Whittaker were teachers and helpers, including Susan Parker, Eleanor ?, Irene Fidler, Mr Hadfield, Len Gregory and Mr and Mrs Hewitt, whose daughter played the part of Mary.

Francis Rigg from Hadfield handled a baby crocodile at a party for workers' children at Maconochies factory in Waterside Mill. In January 1964 Mr Kelly brought several reptiles (this one came in a Bran Flakes box!) from Belle Vue zoo to amuse the children. Quite a change from the usual entertainment of clowns or puppets!

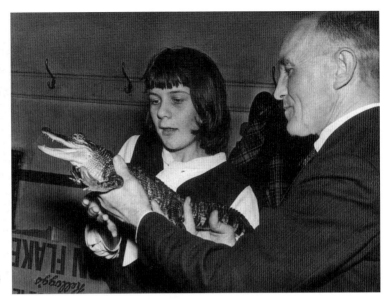

Barbara Castle and Lord Rhodes were the Labour Party speakers at various outdoor locations in and around Glossop during the election campaign in 1964. Mrs Castle appears to have spoken to only a few bystanders on Hadfield Cross and at a time before improvements were made to the Old Hall Square area.

Old houses on Paradise, near Bank Street chapel, had been demolished in 1963. A year later fire spread to furniture when paraffin was used to start the living room fire in this bungalow. A neighbour was rushing to help Mr Gerrard, whose wife unfortunately died from her injuries. The homes on the new Manchester overspill estate are just visible on the right.

First Hadfield Girl Guides celebrated their silver jubilee in November 1965. Former guides, together with their friends and family, were invited to a party in St Andrew's school. There were old photographs and souvenirs from former days on display. Miss Evans, who was the Lieutenant in 1918, cut the cake to mark this momentous occasion.

Miss Minnie Robinson retired in April 1965 after forty years of teaching. She began her career at Whitfield Infants in 1923 before moving to St Andrew's school for the last fourteen years of her working life. Former headmaster Mr Bowden made a presentation, watched by the Revd Whittaker and fellow teachers, including Mrs Booth, Mrs Peggy Davies and Mrs Furlong. Miss Robinson died in 1997, aged 91.

A fire engine travelling towards Glossop had crashed through this wall at Woolley Bridge in July 1965. A local resident surveys the scene from the wooden footbridge over the River Etherow. The old tollhouse is on the left, the newsagents is behind the toppled county sign and the Spread Eagle pub is on the right.

When this North Western bus skidded on Hadfield Road near Hadfield Cross, passengers had to finish their journey on foot. The single-storey butcher's shop just visible at the rear of the bus was owned by the Dewsnap family, who had a field for pigs, sheep and poultry between Walker Street and the Anchor pub on The Smithy.

Children from St Charles Borromeo Roman Catholic church who took their first Communion in around 1965. Amongst the group with Sister Malachy were, from left to right, back row: B. Lee, P. Howard, D. Francomb, -?-, J. O'Driscoll, A. Scorah, G. Howard, P. Revell, G. Reynolds, -?-. Middle row: D. Stokes, S. Cannon, A. Kuczaj, -?-, D. Dalton, -?-, C. Murphy, S. Ferris. Front row: K. Mattimore, S. Williamson, A. Flanagan, C. Howard, C. Marsden, S. Allsop, C. Fuga, S. Thompson, B. Grant, M. McKenna.

nine

1966 & After

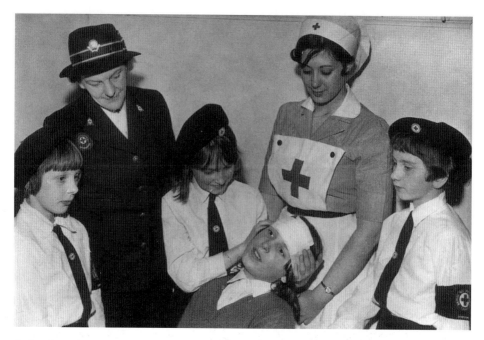

Cadets from the Hadfield branch of the Red Cross demonstrated their skills for the president Mrs Edith Oliver in March 1966. The international organisation was established in 1863 and aims to work for the relief of human suffering regardless of race, colour or creed. In Muslim countries the emblem is a red crescent and in Asia it is a red lion and sun.

Reaching a target of £15,000 was the aim for the fiftieth anniversary of the National Savings movement in 1966. The chairman Mr C. Bowden, who had been awarded the MBE in 1961 for his work encouraging savings, presented his savings book to Jean Wilson at Hadfield post office, watched by the Mayor, Councillor A. Williams and the postmaster Mr J. Woods.

Left: The cenotaph on Remembrance Sunday in November 1966. The war memorial was erected in 1922 to remember those lost in the First World War. It was built two years after the one in Norfolk Square in Glossop, both bearing the winged angel holding a laurel wreath and the words Pro Patria ('For Homeland').

Below: Improvements to Hadfield Cross (to make it like a village green) were completed in 1967. The old cross that gave the square its name is on the left. The first house on the right was once the vicarage, the dentist's surgery is the building partly behind the tree and the three-storey weavers' cottages are lower down Hadfield Road.

Little Red Riding Hood and an artist were just two of the fancy dress contestants at the Rose Queen Festival in the late 1960s. After a procession around the streets the carnival continued with events and the crowning of the queen on the playing fields between New Shaw Lane and Hadfield Road.

Mr and Mrs Bryant (of Waterside in Hadfield) enjoyed a visit from their daughter Hilda Nuryn (who lived in Connecticut, USA) over the Christmas and New Year holiday in 1966. Grandchildren Patricia and Faye were hanging up their stockings for Father Christmas and meeting their grandparents for the first time.

Farm workers from Brook Farm in Padfield had to enlist the help of the fire brigade when a six-year-old Ayrshire cow fell down a culvert in June 1966. Unfortunately it incurred severe injuries and had to be destroyed.

Children from Hadfield schools went by bus to Glossop baths for swimming lessons. These happy children were members of the swimming club in the 1960s. In the centre (with dark curly hair) is Kath Bradley from Queen Street. She later became a swimming instructor and, together with many of her family, was also a member of the Tintwistle brass band.

Most of the side streets in Hadfield were once cobbled and Walker Street was no exception. New kerbstones were being fitted here in preparation for the laying of tarmac over the old sets in 1969.

The Hadfield Artists group relaxed over coffee after staging their exhibition at the community centre in 1969. To encourage new members the group produced a poster which read 'Hadfield Artists, Tuesday at two; Beginners welcome at this centre.'

Hadfield county infants school, 1970/71. From left to right, back row: M. Simmonite, -?-, -?-, S. Hadfield, M. Tonge, L. Judge, K. Eyres, -?-, I. Fitzman. Third row: A. Simmonite, T. Rose, H. Wilton, M. Spencer, C. Ford, G. Savage, L. Ferris, J. Thomasson, Mrs Nuttall and son Gareth. Second row: A. Wild, D. Peacock, K. Worswick, H. Goodwin, P. Rothwell, G. Knight, M. Adams. Front row: -?-. D. Scowcroft, T. Grimshaw, -?-, H. Pilkington, S. Froggatt, S. McKenna, -?-.

The winning football team from St Charles' school in around 1970. From left to right, back row: Andrew Travis, Paul Stephenson, Michael Hirst, Paul Cookney, Andrew Wood, Joey Kuczaj. Front row: James Cunningham, John Mettrick, Robert Clarke, Karl Thompson (with shield), Raymond Nelson (with football), Jonathan Francomb.

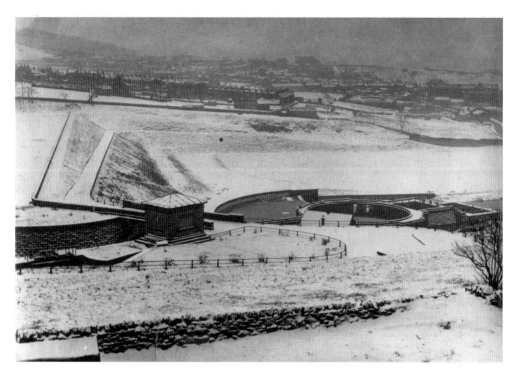

Bottom's reservoir under snow, looking towards Padfield, Brosscroft and Hadfield. On the extreme right is the road past Waterside. Bank Street Chapel can just be seen on the skyline.

Little Padfield is a delightful area near the bottom of Redgate where generations of walkers have meandered past the farms and cottages. Padfield Plum Wakes was celebrated each year as the local plum trees ripened and this tradition was reinstated a few years ago with the Plum Fair. On the right, the tip of Bleaklow is just visible.

St Charles' schoolchildren in around 1970. Father John Sullivan was the parish priest from 1970 to 1999. He was High Peak Dean between 1976 and 1989, a member of the commission for the Pope's visit in 1982 and represented local churches during the twinning with Bad Vibel in Germany in 1986, the same year he wrote a book on the history of the St Charles Borromeo church in Hadfield.

The traditional act of remembrance has taken place on Station Road opposite the Palatine hotel since 1922. Local councillors (including Terry Briody-Duggan, Bert Turner and Ada Williams and Harry Buxton) and uniformed organisations stood for the two minute silence at this service led by the Revd Whittaker in the early 1970s. After 1974, High Peak Council took over from Glossop Borough Council in the area.

St Andrew's school, 1972/73. From left to right, back row: P. Higgins, A. Cartledge, M. Tonge, R. Swindells, M. Weaver, J. Barnes, C. Hayes, S. Davis, M. Robinson. Third row: J. Thomasson, J. Harris, T. Ashworth, T. Foulds, H. Wilton, K. Murry, N. Lomax, H. Pilkington, Mr Murry. Second row: R. Kiffin, I. Fitzman, S. O'Brien, C. Barber, C. Ford, P. Rothwell, A. Elliot, D. Mullet, J. Coleman. First row: D. Scowcroft. S. McKenna, D. Etchells, S. Woodward, T. Grimshaw, L. Ferris, L. Travis, S. Froggatt. Front: D. Peacock. M. Adams, A. Howard.

The Revd Derek W. Bailey was the vicar at St Andrew's from 1973 to 1990. During the church's centenary celebrations in 1972 photographs were displayed on the windowsills. In the centre is a picture of the first incumbent, the Revd Joseph Hadfield, in the window dedicated to him. The Revd Alan Buckley, who ministered in the parish until 2003, succeeded the Revd Bailey.

Pavements were extended down Station Road to create safer crossing points and wider parking bays in the 1990s. On the right is the National Westminster Bank, at the junction with Salisbury Street. Above the station in the centre are the trees of Castle Hill.

Hadfield comprehensive school's first year hockey team, 1975/76. From left to right, back row: Lisa Tollerton, Christine Ford, Wendy Mills, Janet Makinson, Nicolette Lomax, Elaine Brotherton. Front row: Tina O'Brien, Yvonne Ford, Helen Wilton, Katie Murry, Janet Gould, Phillipa Morris, Janet Maley.

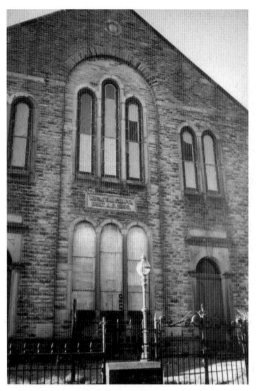

Left: Padfield Wesleyan chapel was built in 1880 on Post Street. James Sargenston laid a memorial stone with a 'time capsule' of coins and local papers buried underneath. In 1997 planning permission was granted to turn the building from a Methodist chapel into apartments. On completion, the penthouse apartment went on sale for a quarter of a million pounds.

Below: A school reunion was organised by Joyce Mitchell and Marjorie Dean for former pupils who started at St Andrew's in 1950, together with their teacher Mrs Davies. Wearing photograph name badges, friendships were renewed at their old school (which is now the Video Vaults) on Railway Street. A cake bearing a picture of the class was cut to mark the occasion.

Former deputy headteacher at Hadfield infant school, Peggy Davies was awarded the MBE in 2004 for her voluntary work over forty years with Glossop Arts Council, the carnival and Victorian weekend, Derbyshire Community Education and the Heritage Centre. Peggy is seen here in one of her beautiful hand-made Victorian dresses outside the Heritage Centre, which she managed for eighteen years.

The Revd Garrie Charles Griffiths became the new vicar at the parish church of St Andrew's on 3 March 2004. He came to Hadfield with his wife Jill after working in several parishes, including the Arctic, Stalybridge, Morton (on the Wirral), Godly (in Hyde) and parishes in Shrewsbury and Suffolk. They have two married sons, Ben and Tom.

Other local titles published by Tempus

Glossop: Volume II
SUE HICKINSON AND MICHAEL H. BROWN

This fascinating collection of over 200 images portrays life in and around the Derbyshire town of Glossop over the last 100 years. There were many photographic studios in the area producing picture postcards featuring idyllic rural scenes, mills, shops, civic events and celebrations. Accompanied by informative captions, this volume will delight all those who have lived and worked in the area, or who have spent time exploring the valleys and dales of this part of Derbyshire.

0 7524 3286 9

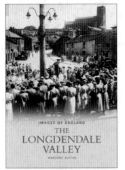

The Longdendale Valley
MARGARET BUXTON

From the eastern outskirts of Manchester through the villages of Mottram, Hollingworth, Hadfield, Tintwhistle, and via reservoirs and open moors to Crowden and the Yorkshire border, the Longdendale Valley wends its windswept way. This book of photographs, mainly taken by the Hadfield photographer Harry Buxton, illustrates a variety of aspects of life in this beautiful valley over the years.

0 7524 3288 5

Denton and Haughton
JILL CRONIN AND THE DENTON LOCAL HISTORY SOCIETY

The neighbouring townships of Denton and Haughton were both famous for hat making but mining, farming and the cotton industry were also important employers in past times. This splendid collection of over 200 old photographs borrowed from local people provides a delightful insight into those times, showing people at work and play through the decades of the twentieth century.

0 7524 0757 0

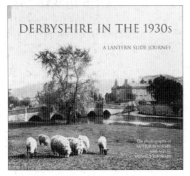

Derbyshire in the 1930s: A lantern slide journey
DONALD ROOKSBY

This beautiful book of photographs takes the reader through some of the most scenic parts of Derbyshire as they looked in the inter-war years. Pastoral scenes of farmland and dale follow views of towns and villages, and the county town itself, all looking quieter and calmer than they do today. The photographs were all taken originally to be used as lantern slides to entertain audiences in village halls around the county.

0 7524 3258 3

If you are interested in purchasing other books published by Tempus, or in case you have difficulty finding any Tempus books in your local bookshop, you can also place orders directly through our website

www.tempus-publishing.com